Ugly Crying in a Bed Bath and Beyond

Nicole Siciliano

BookLeaf Publishing
India | USA | UK

Ugly Crying in a Bed Bath and Beyond ©
2023 Nicole Siciliano

All rights reserved.

Presentation by *BookLeaf Publishing*

Web: www.bookleafpub.com

E-mail: info@bookleafpub.com

ISBN: 9789357215565

First edition 2023

This one is for me.

ACKNOWLEDGEMENT

I would like to thank every friend, peer and professor who has read anything I've ever written, no matter how whiny, and not rolled their eyes.

Thank you to my mother, for saving all of my literary triumphs from the fourth grade. First drafts are undoubtedly the foundation for good writing, and I will forever be grateful that you file everything.

To my friends, who called me a writer, even during the years when the pen didn't touch the page, I am lucky to have you.

To anyone who has gotten caught in the crosshairs of the editing process during this 21-day challenge and didn't scare off too easily, a big thank you.

PREFACE

Love is a kaleidoscope. It's always changing and it never quite looks the same, no matter how many times you try to turn the lens just right. I guess I've been pretty lucky to learn this.

When I think about poetry, I often think about photography. Some people can appreciate a sunset or a wide-lensed landscape for what it is. But for me, art is boring without the complexity of people in the frame – their joy, sadness, flaws and passions front and center..

I've had some time to think about what this collection means to me, and at the end of the day, it's about people. More specifically, this book is about the people that I love, while reckoning with the imperfectness of being human – the complicated mirror that is a family, the profoundness that is friendship, the lessons learned from those who have come and gone, and even the life-long journey of living with myself.

I don't believe in looking at the world through a lens of superficial optimism, but I do believe there is beauty in the grit and that there is something uniquely great in accepting things for exactly how they are. Maybe that's even more worthwhile.

I hope you read this collection and see that too, no matter which way the lens turns. I hope that even through the sadness, the restlessness, the touches of loss and the quiet of contentment, you can see that love is there too.

And of course, as the title suggests, I hope you can appreciate the touch of dark humor.

Burn This

My parents raised me better
than to trade the family [secrets]
for a chance at a soul.

Inheritance

I am

three generations of rotting olive branches,
slamming screen doors, shotgun shells.

I wear this name like a punch
line I can't take off. Tell me,

am I

the rust on your iron fist, the knife
between your teeth   shining like a *fuck you,*

the gravel in your throat that grew
the perfect white oleander

of my mother?

Tuesday Night; 11:58 PM

3

Tonight, the houseplant and I
aren't doing so hot.

One of us is dehydrated,
the other is just depressed

again.

We wilt together in the blue
frames of another infomercial

and I can't remember which one
I'm supposed to be.

So, I reach for another bottle, crack it
as wide as my father smiles

and almost remember
the good times.

An Apology to the Happiest Days

I'm sorry.

Sometimes, my sadness gets stuck between my
teeth, and I can't say anything with a smile.

But I remember how
we carried the beach home in our shoes,

the way-way back of the family
station wagon and

counting cornfields on road trips
through Pennsylvania.

In our house, there were gold stars
on spelling tests, new tap shoes,

Christmas gifts, birthday candles,
drivers ed and a brass saxophone.

There were games nights, dance nights,
Easy-Bake Oven nights, night-swimming nights,

crafts nights, milkshake nights

build-a-fort nights, catch-a-firefly-nights,

Blockbuster Video nights.

And sometimes, there were even nights
we all remembered to be happy.

Writing Your Eulogy Across from You at the Bar

You were so gorgeous,

dancing in the high

beams of a speeding car.

Science is a Real Motherfucker

There are 14,000 cellphone towers in this city,

but the dial tone between us drip-drip-dripped,
until it rusted like a leaking faucet.

Did you know bones are 30 percent water?

You'd leave drinking glasses on the nightstand
and I managed to break those too.

Einstein said energy cannot be created or
destroyed.

So, I've been reading up on necromancy, trying
to learn the art of reanimating things long dead.

The human skeleton regenerates every 10 years.

I mark the days on the calendar and think,
is there anything left of you that used to hold
me?

Ugly Crying in a Bed Bath and Beyond

When my grandfather died,
my grandmother slept with his pillow.

For 10 years,

even after the sheets were washed,
she swore she could still smell him.

Then she died too.

I can't stop thinking about that
as I fall asleep on your side of the bed.

You are not dead.
You are just somewhere

else.

But I've been trying to calculate the
mathematical probability of seeing your face

in a passing subway car,

and I know you are just as gone
as the saddest branches on my family tree.

Sometimes, I still count

the windows in the skyscrapers
that lead to your last known address.

I stain my teeth with all your favorite vices.

I do the crossword on Sundays,
I watch the news.

I bought new sheets yesterday.

I Snake Your Hair from the Drain Six Months after the Breakup

How long will it take until the New York City Crime Scene

Investigation Unit can no longer find evidence of a body

that walked itself out the door?

On Spite and Midcentury Architecture

I clench your name between my teeth
and it breaks my jaw,

but I've learned it's better to chew gravel
than to spit rocks.

I know I live in a glass house,
I built it myself.

I just got your fingerprints
off the door.

Gone Fishing

12

There were whole years
I couldn't write a single poem.
I was too busy being happy.

Watermarks

He holds me in the middle of the night,

like he knows there are ghosts lurking in the
closet
and he's just waiting to hear the doorknob turn.

But I have never been good at folding dirty
laundry, or neatly hanging the past like a heretic.

So, I wear it like a necklace of baby teeth.

I hum it like the music box
that holds the family secrets.

And we just live like that,

with the dying plants on the windowsill,
the stale wine in the refrigerator,

the not-quite-right-hum
of the radiator.

My love, there is nothing
that will snatch you in the middle of the night.

There are no waiting skeletons to dance with.
There is just the creak of my own bones

in the morning

and the beer bottle watermarks
of a far-away life on the nightstand.

Sunday Social Club

15

Tonight, laughter salts the rim of the glass,
the lights are dim and the neighborhood
barflies call for one more round.

Postcard from Lisbon, 2017

We choked on blue smoke
in the belly of an after-after hours club,

finally emerged with the morning joggers
and found our way home.

We drank sweet red blends and slept
until the November afternoon was already gray.

We didn't see a single museum, just the white
linen tablecloths at the seaside,

shelling fresh clams in olive oil,
baking in the salt and autumn sun.

I called it our lost week, as we
ran for our connection back home,

and maybe it was, as the days
ran together like bad grammar,

I didn't know how to say thank you.

Tonight, I think of you in the yellow lamplight,
from somewhere in New York City,

the salt and smoke still in your hair,
the feeling of being alive

caught between your teeth,

and I smile.

My Body, in Memoriam

18

Friend, it has been 13 years since you've been gone. I watched the days blur together like smoke in the bar light.

Can you forgive me for growing older? I carry your name in my aching hip bones, and I walk among the living.

Confession

I write about love like it's both
the graveyard and the shovel,

a ghost in the doorframe,
the whole haunted house.

And it's unfair to you,
warm body in the bed,

your breath, soft
on my neck in the dark,

your toothbrush next to mine
in the next room over.

In the afternoons, I watch
you water the houseplants.

I read once that succulents
like the sound of laughter.

When we are happiest,
I want to plant seeds

beneath the floorboards,
watch them grow wild

and easy, as my shoes
on your doorstep,

the coffeepot timer, your
wristwatch and it's gentle

tick tick tick. I know
love it for the living.

When I Say I Spent a Summer at Magic Camp

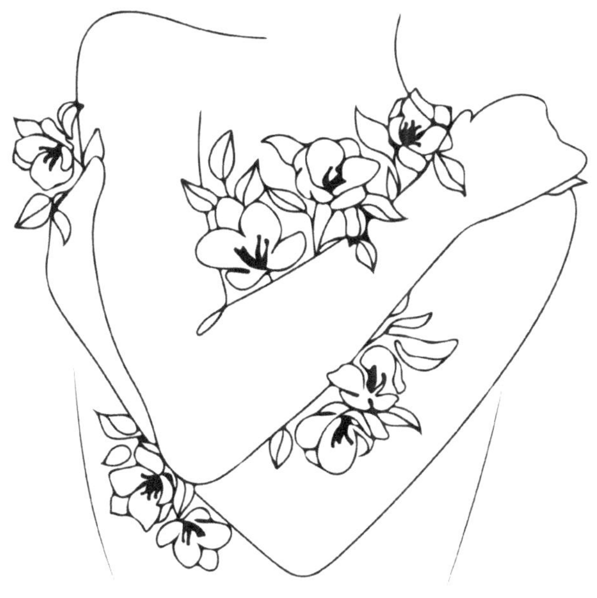

I want to tell you about the years
I tried to make my own body disappear.

All so I could stand on a stage, in a
classroom, a subway platform, a job interview

and someone would believe
I was worthy of applause.

Sometimes, I still feel for the sharp
of my hip bones like the corners on a trap door.

More often than I want to admit,
I think about pulling the cord.

For my next act, watch me stay.

For Maggie, Age Two

I never knew my grandmother
but they say she had a knife for a tongue,

that she left this world the same
way she entered it *swinging.*

Nobody fucked with Margaret.

I know I'm supposed to want you
to grow up to be kind,

and I do,

but I hope you find your bite,
your snarl, the sharp

on your knuckle
if you ever need to throw a fist.

I hope you never take anybody's bullshit.

Maggie, people are mostly good,
until sometimes they're not.

I don't want you to know that yet,

but there will be

school-bus bullies, fairweather friends, men

who look right through you

and worse.

Tonight, I watch you move
through rooms unafraid to break things.

Keep swinging.

Write the Poem Tomorrow

Let today be for drinking coffee
without a metaphor,

scraping butter on toast, warm
socks pulled from the dryer, dog-eared

paperbacks and the tongues
of old running shoes.

Let today be for the wrong subway line
without symbolism,

Breath fogged on glass, winter
hats shoved into pockets, the cold

of a red apple between teeth and white
pages in a notebook for another day.